Journeys

—

Our lives are filled with journeys of both the outer and inner kinds. The two sorts need a journal to capture them. Sometimes, we'll be recording a trip around the Cape of Good Hope or five days in Rome. At other times, without anything mystical being meant by this, we'll be involved in tracking an inner journey: a trip towards a different kind of relationship with our work, our families or our partners.

Both physical and emotional journeys need careful monitoring, or we are likely to become lost, directionless and forgetful.

We need to record the most significant moments that befall us: the surprise we feel in a new place (it might be the mountains behind Tokyo or the shores of the Bosphorus) or in front of a new idea or emotion (perhaps we're just reading Lao-Tze or properly falling in love for the first time, with our child or a partner).

We should appreciate the triumphs and the difficulties of our journeys – just as a climber might record how they endured a blizzard, or what they learned from a fall.

A journal is a small, elegant tool that makes up for our endemic forgetfulness. It sums up mental and physical travel; it gives longer life to fleeting inspirations and sensations; it decodes experiences; it preserves the treasures we have stumbled upon along the way. It will stand as a record of who we are.

What we often crave from our travels are souvenirs. But good souvenirs are desperately thin on the ground. When we go on trips, gift shops will push on us miniature camels or plastic Eiffel Towers. When we retire after a lifetime at the office, we're given a framed photo or else we mark the journey to university graduation with a gown and a certificate. We need better than this.

What we need, above all, are records of sensations and ideas. We need to be able to read, many years from now, about what we felt and how it marked us. This is a place to jot down where we have been, in our minds and on the earth – and why it mattered.